# Stories of
# the Blessed
# Sacrament

Under the direction of Romain Lizé, Executive Vice President, MAGNIFICAT
Editor, MAGNIFICAT: Isabelle Galmiche
Editor, Ignatius: Vivian Dudro
Translator: Janet Chevrier
Proofreader: Claire Gilligan
Assistant to the Editor: Pascale van de Walle
Layout Designers: Armelle Riva, Jean-Marc Richard
Production: Thierry Dubus, Sabine Marioni

Original French edition: *Les belles histoires de ma communion*
© 2018 by Mame, Paris.
© 2019 by MAGNIFICAT, New York • Ignatius Press, San Francisco
All rights reserved.

FRANCINE BAY – HENGJING ZANG

# Stories of the Blessed Sacrament

MAGNIFICAT · Ignatius

# Contents

The Bread in the Desert . . . . . . . . . . . . . . . . . . . . . . . . . . . . . . 7

The Multiplication of the Loaves. . . . . . . . . . . . . . . . . . . . . . . . . 13

The Last Supper . . . . . . . . . . . . . . . . . . . . . . . . . . . . . . . . . . . . 21

On the Road to Emmaus . . . . . . . . . . . . . . . . . . . . . . . . . . . . . 28

Saint Tarcisius . . . . . . . . . . . . . . . . . . . . . . . . . . . . . . . . . . . . . 37

Saint Anthony's Mule . . . . . . . . . . . . . . . . . . . . . . . . . . . . . . . 45

Saint Thomas Aquinas . . . . . . . . . . . . . . . . . . . . . . . . . . . . . . 51

Fire! Fire! . . . . . . . . . . . . . . . . . . . . . . . . . . . . . . . . . . . . . . . . 59

Saint Margaret Mary Alacoque. . . . . . . . . . . . . . . . . . . . . . . . . 67

Secret Mass in a French Forest . . . . . . . . . . . . . . . . . . . . . . . . 75

Saint Pius X, the Pope of the Blessed Sacrament . . . . . . . . . . . 83

The Secret Ordination at Dachau. . . . . . . . . . . . . . . . . . . . . . . 89

What a wonderful gift,

to receive the Sacrament of the Eucharist!

Through his love,

Jesus offers himself to you, to us.

These twelve lovely stories

will help you to enter even more deeply

into the mystery of this beautiful Sacrament,

which Jesus left us to keep us close to him.

# The Bread in the Desert

*Based on Exodus 16*

In the dead of night, led by Moses, the Hebrews made their escape from Egypt, where they had been the slaves of Pharaoh.

Early the next morning, Pharaoh ordered his army, "Quick, after them! You must catch them!"

They immediately hitched up their chariots and set out in hot pursuit. But, just as God had promised Moses, he protected the Hebrews. He parted the Red Sea for them, and the Egyptians drowned when the water rushed back into place.

How happy the Hebrews were to be free at last and on their way home to the Promised Land, the land that God had given to their ancestors Abraham, Isaac, and Jacob! But their journey through the desert was hard: it was very hot, there was little water, and food was scarce.

After two months, the tired and hungry Hebrews became angry with Moses.

"Why did you bring us out of Egypt?" they cried. "There at least we could sit down around our big pots of stew, and we had all the bread we could eat, to say nothing of the fish, the melons, the cucumbers.... Now, thanks to you, we are all going to starve here in the desert!"

God heard the complaints of the poor Hebrews and said to Moses, "I will rain down bread from heaven for you. Every morning, when the Hebrews come out of their tents, they will find their daily bread lying on the ground. In the evening, I will send them meat to eat."

While announcing the good news to everyone, Moses said, "Now you must see that God himself freed you from slavery in Egypt and that he is still watching over you. You will have meat this very evening, and in the morning, as much bread as you need!"

The Hebrews wondered how that could possibly be when, suddenly, flocks of quail entered the camp. What a miracle! The people roasted the birds with herbs, and a delicious aroma filled the air. Everyone joined in the feast. Things were finally looking up!

The next morning, the camp was covered with dew. As it evaporated, a fine, flaky bread-like stuff was left on the ground.

"What is it? What is it?" the Hebrews kept asking.

In Hebrew, this question is pronounced "*Man-hu*?" And so it was that this strange bread became known as "manna." But what was this manna like?

The Hebrews found it delicious and very nourishing, with a little taste of honey.

Moses said to them, "Gather up as much as you need according to the number of people in your family. But you must not store up any for tomorrow, for God will provide enough for each day!"

Some, wishing to stock up, disobeyed Moses. And the next day, the manna they had saved for later was rotten and ridden with worms.

There was one exception to the rule against gathering extra manna. "On the sixth day of the week, everyone must collect a double ration," Moses said, "for on the seventh day—the day consecrated to the Lord—you must do no work.  On that day there will be no manna on the ground."

So it was that, during the whole forty years it took the Hebrews to cross the desert, six days a week, they gathered all the manna they needed to satisfy their hunger.

God took care of his people: he fed them and strengthened them. So that future generations would know the goodness of the Lord, God told the Hebrews to fill a jar with manna and to keep it as proof of his faithfulness to them.

This golden jar was kept with the tablets of the Ten Commandments in the ark of the covenant.

Today, we are like the Hebrews in the desert. We are making a journey to our true homeland—heaven. And, along the way, God feeds us and cares for us with bread from heaven: the Eucharist!

# The Multiplication of the Loaves

*Based on Matthew 14:13-21,*
*Mark 6:34-44, Luke 9:10-17,*
*and John 6:1-13*

Young Martialis had been struggling along the rocky pathway. The sack of food he carried grew heavier with every step. Reaching a clearing, Martialis looked out at the Sea of Galilee. And he stared at the biggest crowd of people he had ever seen. They covered every inch of the shoreline and the grassy hill.

"Martialis! Come with us!" two voices called out.

Martialis was relieved that his cousins had found him. Together they made their way close to the shore.

"Jesus is already here," said his cousins. "He is healing people! Look!"

Nearby, the sick and the lame lay where friends had placed them. Some cried out, "Jesus, have mercy on me! Jesus, heal me!"

Martialis watched in amazement. With great tenderness, Jesus laid hands on the people and prayed over them. And they were healed!

Jesus had come here to pray and to rest with his disciples. But his heart filled with compassion when he saw the great number of people. Jesus knew they were like sheep without a shepherd.

Jesus told the people to sit. Then he talked of the Kingdom of God.

"Happy are the pure of heart, for they will see God," Jesus promised. "Happy are the peacemakers, for they will be called children of God."

The crowd listened eagerly, hungry to hear what Jesus had to say.

Young Martialis was deeply moved by the goodness that radiated from Jesus. His heart burned with excitement as Jesus spoke. As he listened, Martialis felt himself becoming a better person. He wanted to follow Jesus and do as he said. He wanted to stay with the Lord forever.

As evening neared, Martialis could feel his eyelids drooping. It was getting late. Here and there, little children started crying for something to eat. The adults, too, grew restless.

Philip and some of the other Apostles went to Jesus and said, "Master, send this crowd away to the nearby villages and farms to find something to eat. They are tired and hungry."

But Jesus replied, "There is no need for them to leave. Give them food yourselves."

Philip sighed and said, "It would take a small fortune to feed a crowd as big as this." For there were thousands of people.

Martialis was suddenly wide awake. His heart beat wildly with excitement. He turned to Andrew the Apostle, who sat nearby.

"I have these," Martialis said, showing Andrew the contents of his sack.

Andrew went to Jesus and said, "There is a boy here who has five barley loaves and two fish. But what good are they for so many people?"

With a friendly smile, Jesus motioned for Martialis to come near. Martialis emptied his sack at Jesus' feet.

"Have everyone sit down," Jesus told his Apostles. He took the loaves of bread, raised his eyes to heaven, and blessed them. Next, he broke the loaves into pieces and had the disciples hand them out to the crowd. Then he did the same with the fish.

That's when an extraordinary thing happened. As the food was distributed to the people, it multiplied. People ate and ate until they were filled.

"But there were only five loaves and two fish!" exclaimed Martialis. "How is it possible that it was enough for all these people?"

When everyone had eaten their fill, Jesus said to his Apostles, "Collect all the fragments left over, so that nothing is wasted."

The Apostles came back with twelve baskets full.

Martialis could hardly believe his eyes. His small gift of five loaves and two fish had fed more than five thousand people! The young boy had witnessed what we believe: that whatever we give to the Lord, he transforms and multiplies.

At every Eucharist, we bring Jesus our gifts of bread and wine. And we give him our very selves, too. Then he transforms the bread and the wine into his own Body and Blood, which makes us who receive them more and more like him.

That very day, Martialis made up his mind to follow Jesus. And he did just that.

According to holy legend, a grown-up Martialis was sent by Saint Peter to evangelize the southwest of ancient Gaul, modern-day France. There he is known as Saint Martial, the first bishop of Limoges. And people still tell the tale of that saint of humble yet amazing beginnings—of that boy whose generous act led to the multiplication of the loaves and the fishes!

# The Last Supper

*Based on Mark 14:12-31 and John 13*

The Apostles Peter and John hurried through one of the great gates into Jerusalem. Yesterday, they had asked Jesus, "Where would you like us to prepare the Passover meal?"

Jesus had replied, "Go into the city. There you will find a man carrying a jug of water. Follow him, and at the house he enters, tell the owner that I wish to celebrate Passover there."

And, indeed, just as they entered the city they saw a man walking in front of them carrying a jug of water. They followed him into the large courtyard of a house. They had no trouble finding Marcus, busy with his servants filling jars with oil.

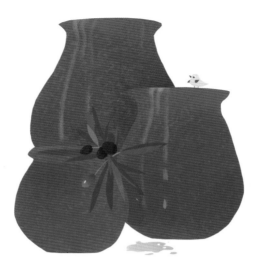

Peter spoke up: "Hello, Marcus! The Master, Jesus, wishes to celebrate the Passover meal at your house."

Straightaway, Marcus led them upstairs to a large room furnished with cushions. All was just as Jesus had said, so Peter and John prepared for the Passover meal without delay.

When it was evening, Jesus arrived at the house with the other Apostles. They sat down at table, but before beginning to eat, Jesus got up, took off his cloak, and tied a towel around his waist. He poured some water into a basin and began washing his disciples' feet, exactly as servants did. Then he dried them with the towel.

When his turn came, Peter was outraged: "You, Lord, you want to wash my feet?! No, never!"

But Jesus gently replied, "You don't know now what I am doing, but later you will understand."

So Peter finally gave in and let him wash his feet.

Then Jesus put his robe back on and returned to his place at table. He explained to his friends, his Apostles, "I have set you an example: you too ought to wash one another's feet. The greatest in the Kingdom of God is the one who is the servant of others."

Jesus and his Apostles began to eat. But this Passover meal was unlike any other: it was to be Jesus' last meal with his friends. He knew that he was soon to die; this was a truly dark hour. But what was most heartbreaking for Jesus was knowing that Judas was about to hand him over to his enemies for thirty pieces of silver. The meal had just begun when Jesus sorrowfully declared, "Truly, I say to you, one of you will betray me."

The Apostles looked at one another, wondering who could do such a thing. They too became very sorrowful as, one by one, they asked, "Could he mean me?" When Judas in turn said, "Could it be me?" Jesus replied with a heavy heart, "It is you who says so." And with that, Judas left. Night was already falling.

Before his death, Jesus wished to leave his friends—and all of us too—a true treasure, the greatest gift ever. He wished to give all he had, his very self.

So he took the bread on the table, blessed it, raised it in his hands, and lifted his eyes to heaven. Then he gave some to each of them, saying, "Take this and eat; this is my body."

Then he took the cup of wine that was also on the table. He prayed in the same way, and said, "Take this, all of you, and drink of it. This is my blood, which will be poured out for you and for many for the forgiveness of sins."

The Apostles, who had been following Jesus for a long time and had seen all the wonders he had done, understood that he was the Son of God. They knew that what Jesus had just said was true, even if his words were a bit mysterious.

Their hearts were overflowing with love, and even more so when Jesus added, "Do this in memory of me."

Ever since that day, the Apostles and their successors, that is, bishops and priests, have faithfully repeated this act of Jesus, just as he asked. This is what we call Mass. When we go to Communion, like the Apostles on the night of the Last Supper, we receive the Body and Blood of Jesus. The consecrated host is Jesus himself, who comes to dwell in our hearts!

# On the Road to Emmaus

*Based on Luke 24:13-35*

"Psst, Cleopas, meet me on the other side of the hill!"

"Right, see you later!" Cleopas answered.

Walking at a brisk pace, the two friends met up outside the walls of Jerusalem, away from the hubbub of the city. In these troubled times, they didn't want to risk being seen together, for they were disciples of Jesus of Nazareth. After Jesus' crucifixion on Mount Golgotha two days earlier, it wasn't safe to be known as one of his friends. The high priest had even forbidden giving food or shelter to followers of Jesus! The two companions had decided to flee Jerusalem, and they were on their way to the pretty village of Emmaus.

"Come on," said Cleopas to his friend, "a long walk in the countryside will do us good after everything that's just happened."

"I hope you're right, Cleopas. I feel terrible," his friend answered. "I can't believe what our leaders did to Jesus, condemning him like a common criminal and handing him over to our Roman rulers to be crucified!"

"Yes, I feel the same," Cleopas agreed. "Like you, I had believed that Jesus would free us from the Romans."

"Especially given all the amazing miracles we saw him do!" his friend added.

Weighed down with sadness, Cleopas and his companion had slowed their pace. When they arrived at a crossroads, they took the road to Emmaus. They still had several miles to go before they would reach the village.

Suddenly, they noticed a man approaching from behind.

"Let's slow down a little and let him pass by," whispered Cleopas.

When the man caught up to them, he asked, "What were you talking about along the way? You seem so sad."

Cleopas and his friend stopped, a little amazed. "You must be the only person in Jerusalem who hasn't heard what's been happening there these past couple of days!"

"What's that, then?" the man asked.

"Well, what happened to Jesus of Nazareth, of course! Before God and all the people, that man showed his might through his words and deeds. But our leaders condemned him to death and handed him over to the Romans to be crucified. We had been hoping that he would free our land, but now it's already two days since this all happened."

With a great sigh, Cleopas went on, "We're still overwhelmed by what some women in our group have told us: they went to the tomb early this morning but couldn't find the body of Jesus! They said that angels appeared who announced that Jesus was alive! Our friends went to see for themselves. They found the tomb empty, but Jesus they did not see."

"Oh, my poor friends," replied their mysterious companion. "How slow you are to believe all that had been foretold by the prophets! Did the Christ not have to suffer all this in order to one day enter into his glory?"

And, beginning with Moses, he explained to them all that had been foretold in the books of the Old Testament about the suffering Messiah.

Cleopas and his companion were deeply moved as they listened to him. The man's words were captivating!

Night had begun to fall when the first houses of Emmaus at last came into view. The man made as though he would continue on his way, but Cleopas and his friend insisted, "Stay with us, for it is late and night is falling!"

So the three of them entered an inn on the edge of the village and sat down to eat after their long walk.

While they were at table, the man took the bread before him, blessed it, broke it, and gave it to them.

That's when Cleopas and his friend realized who the man was! He was Jesus!

But Jesus immediately vanished from their sight. How great was their joy! So it was true that he was alive! They said to each other, "Weren't our hearts burning within us as we listened to him along the road explaining the Scriptures?"

Overjoyed, they immediately set out to return to Jerusalem, despite the late hour. When they rejoined the Apostles, they recounted what had happened along the road, and how they had recognized Jesus in the breaking of the bread.

"The Lord is truly risen," they rejoiced, "alleluia!"

# Saint Tarcisius

In the early morning silence, a great thud suddenly clattered on the big paving stones of the Appian Way, south of Rome. Hiding in the branches of a cypress, Marcus had just jumped down from the tree. He'd been on the lookout for his friend for a while now, and was pleased to take him by surprise.

"Hi, Tarcisius! I bet I gave you a scare!"

"Hey, Marcus! It's great to see you!"

The two boys, both eight years old, were excited to see each other; they hadn't met since Marcus' baptism two weeks before.

Within a few minutes, the boys reached a little grotto behind the trees and started down a long underground stairway.

"Wow! Forty-three steps!" shouted Marcus, who was still fairly new to this mysterious place that people would later call the catacombs.

Tarcisius led his friend down a long, dark tunnel. In the walls, they could make out recesses covered with marble or wooden plaques bearing inscriptions and drawings of an anchor, a fish, or some other secret symbol known only to Christians.

Tarcisius explained to his friend, "Those are Christian tombs. We come here to be with our faithful departed, to pray with them and for them."

"Wait for me! I can barely see a thing!" cried Marcus a little fearfully. Fortunately, an oil lamp in a corner cast a little light.

They arrived at last in a kind of cave, well lit by torches. Twenty or so people were gathered there. The priest Demetrius, clothed in a large white and gold cope, was about to celebrate Mass.

"You see the altar, Marcus? That's the tomb of a martyr who died for Christ! I'm going to leave you now; I have to go get ready because I'm serving at Mass."

Soon, beautiful chants rose up from two choirs. It was truly magnificent! Then the priest read a long passage from the Gospel, followed by a prayer: "You have called us, Lord, from darkness into light, from ignorance to knowledge of your glory. Blessed are you, for you have opened our hearts to know you, the one true God!"

Mass took place in an atmosphere of great devotion. Tarcisius stood right next to the priest, paying careful attention. Marcus watched his friend with admiration.

The priest urged the faithful: "Let us pray to almighty God with all our hearts for our brothers and sisters who, as I speak, are imprisoned by the emperor because they are Christians. Give them the strength, Lord, to witness to their faith without faltering. May their example encourage us, and ever be a reminder to us that true life is in heaven with you, Lord God! And may we, my brothers and sisters, always be ready to witness to the truth right to the end, even when persecuted, lest our house be swept away by storms like a house built on sand!"

Next, everyone rose to recite the Creed with great fervor. Who knew if tomorrow they might be asked to give up their life for professing their faith!

After more hymns, this little flock of Christians exchanged a kiss of peace before receiving Communion in great silence and with deep emotion. Finally, everyone knelt to receive Demetrius' blessing, wondering if perhaps it might be the last.

After the closing prayer, Demetrius' clear voice rang out: "Is there anyone among you, brothers, brave enough to carry the Blessed Sacrament to our very dear friends in prison, Agapit, Claudius, Stephen, and Lucius? They are soon to be thrown to the lions and put to death. It is so important to them to receive Jesus!"

Hardly had he finished speaking when the little voice of Tarcisius piped up, "Me, me! Oh, Father, let me carry Jesus to our brothers!"

"You, Tarcisius?! But you're far too young!"

"Exactly, Father, they'll let me through. No one will pay any attention to me! Oh, let me take Jesus! I will hold him so tight to my heart the whole way that no one will be able to take him from me!"

Demetrius was deeply touched. "Go then, my child," he said. "Take Jesus, and may God go with you!"

Bidding Marcus farewell, Tarcisius set off on his secret mission to Rome.

He walked quickly, hugging his treasure tightly. He was soon in sight of the great Porta Capena, the city gate not far from the prison. That's when some playmates who weren't Christians recognized him and called out, "Tarcisius, come play with us; we need you on our team!"

Obviously, Tarcisius couldn't stop to play. But they insisted, "Oh, come on! But first, what's that you're holding so tight?"

Tarcisius tried to walk faster. But the group of boys caught up with him, making fun of him and jostling him, trying to grab what he was holding. Suddenly, spotting the host, one of them cried out with scorn, "He's a Christian!"

They instantly threw themselves on him, punching and kicking him. When he was on the ground, they began pelting him with big stones.

Tarcisius knew he was about to die, and he begged Jesus, "Don't fall into their hands, Jesus, flee!"

He was left lying on the ground, with bloodied head and arms, when Quadratus, a Roman soldier who was secretly a Christian, came upon him. He took him in his arms to carry him to a priest.

Brave little Tarcisius died before he could get there. Yet, in his bloody hands, he was still clutching to his heart the linen pouch with the Eucharist.

But when the priest opened the pouch, it was empty! Jesus was no longer there! What a great mystery—his Body, in the host, had completely united with that of this little martyr as he fell asleep in death.

# Saint Anthony's Mule

Saint Francis of Assisi was a great friend of nature. He saw the work of God in every creature. At the first rays of dawn, he would joyously cry out, "Good morning, brother sun!" To the birds gathered on the nearby branches, he said, "Good morning, my friends, have you slept well?" He even greeted the insects. "And you, little sister ladybug, have you already had a nice little walk this morning?"

One day, Francis sent his friend whom we now know as Saint Anthony of Padua on a mission to the south of France. "You speak well," Francis said. "You must go change the hearts of the people there who refuse to believe in God."

Like Francis, Anthony loved talking to the animals. One day, in an Italian port, he even gave a beautiful sermon to a shoal of fish, who all raised their heads above the water to hear him!

Anthony also knew how to touch the hearts of men through his fine words.

He arrived in the French city of Toulouse, where the people gathered in great numbers to listen to him.

"Come, my friends," he said to them, "come into the church to worship Jesus present in the Eucharist! Even if all you see is the host, don't you realize it is Jesus himself there, waiting for you, holding out his arms to take you to his heart?"

Everyone was very impressed by Anthony's words. But one peasant, Zachary Guillard, who was passing by with his mule, abruptly interrupted him: "No, no, a thousand times no! I don't believe a word of your stories! I won't believe it until I see it with my own eyes!"

"My friend," Anthony replied, "no matter what people say about mules, even they're not as stubborn as you are! What would you say if your mule bowed down before the host?"

"Ha!" laughed Zachary. "Now there's a thought!" And he suggested a bargain to Anthony: "I won't give my mule a thing to eat for three days. On the third day, I'll bring her here to the town square. I'll put a big bucket of the fresh oats she loves on one side of her, and you show her your host on the other! You can bet she'll go right for the oats!"

And he broke out in laughter! He was so sure of himself, he added, "If she refuses the oats and bows down before the host, well, then I'll believe!"

Anthony had perfect faith in Jesus and, through experience, knew that animals were God's creatures who, in their simplicity, could understand things that men, in their pride, could not. Still this was a curious kind of bargain!

He prayed with all his heart until the great day arrived.

The shops were closed and the streets were deserted, for everyone was waiting in the town square. Zachary arrived pulling his mule, who hadn't eaten for three days and looked exhausted. Anthony came out of the church carrying the Blessed Sacrament. In plain view, across from the church, the bucket of oats was ready. A great hush descended on the square, and all eyes were fixed on Zachary's mule. What would she do? Without hesitation, and with firm footing, she went straight up to the host and—miracle of miracles—she knelt down as though it were the most natural thing in the world while staring at the host with her big black eyes!

The crowd erupted with joy: "Alleluia, alleluia, the mule chose Jesus! For he is truly there, alive, in the host!"

Zachary Guillard was as good as his word: stunned, he went down on his knees before the host.

"Forgive me, Father Anthony," he murmured. "Yes, I now believe that it is truly Jesus himself present in the host. My mule understood that before me; she has shown me what I refused to accept."

Anthony blessed him with all his heart. Then, turning to the mule, still kneeling in adoration, he added, "Rise, my sweet sister mule, and come eat the big bucket of oats prepared for you by your master!"

Tradition has it that Zachary was baptized, taking the name Pierre. A church in Bourges, France, bears the name Saint Pierre-le-Guillard in memory of the miracle of the mule. There is a painting and even a sculpture there of the animal on its knees.

# Saint Thomas Aquinas

There were wonderful, mouth-watering platters set on the king's table. The king, Saint Louis, was hosting a dinner in honor of some very important people. Among them was Saint Thomas Aquinas, a young Dominican. He was a very learned man, and because he was big and strong, and spoke very few words, his classmates had called him "the dumb ox."

Conversation was in full flow when, suddenly, a great fist thumped down on the table, rattling the platters and making the guests jump. "I've got it! At last, I've found an argument no man can deny!" shouted Thomas, clearly so lost in his thoughts he'd forgotten where he was.

All eyes turned to the king, expecting his displeasure, but the king's face lit up with a bright smile. He immediately ordered one of the servants, "Quick! Fetch a scribe to note down Thomas' argument before he forgets it!"

It's clear to see, Thomas Aquinas was always looking for ways to make the Faith better understood, even while at dinner with a king! So it is no surprise that when many Christians were arguing over the nature of the Eucharist, they turned to Thomas to ask for his opinion.

In his reply that night, after the dinner, Thomas wrote that Jesus is truly present in the Eucharist. Prior to sending it, he went inside a church to pray before the tabernacle, where the consecrated hosts are kept.

A witness said that he heard a voice saying to Thomas, "You have written well about me, my son. What would you like as a reward?"

Thomas' heartfelt reply burst out, "Oh, only you, Lord!"

Thomas would soon have another opportunity to show his great love of the Eucharist.

At Cornillon Abbey in Belgium, there lived a young nun named Juliana. Night after night she had been having the same strange dream: in the middle of a beautiful starry sky was a brilliant round moon, but part of it was always mysteriously dark. In her prayers, she begged to know what this vision could mean.

Jesus answered her, "The Church is missing a feast day in honor of the Eucharist."

Sister Juliana told all of this to her confessor, Father Jacques Pantaléon, who at the time didn't take her very seriously. He said, "We already have the feast day of Holy Thursday for the Eucharist."

Some time later, Father Jacques became Pope Urban IV. During his papacy, a great miracle occurred in Bolsena, Italy: a priest saw blood coming from the host in his hands at Mass. After checking out the story for himself, Urban IV was convinced it was true. That's when Sister Juliana's words came again to his mind.

The pope summoned Thomas Aquinas, a man he deeply admired, and said, "Brother Thomas, I would like to reward you for all your writings, and wish to appoint you bishop of Naples."

"Oh, Holy Father," Thomas replied, "please put any such thought from your mind! Such an honor is not for me. If you will allow me, I would prefer a thousand times more that you declare a feast day in honor of the Holy Eucharist!"

How could the pope resist? In 1264, he instituted what is now known as the Solemnity of the Most Holy Body and Blood of Christ (*Corpus Christi*). Then he proposed a competition to Thomas Aquinas and his Franciscan friend Saint Bonaventure to compose prayers for this new feast day. Both men prayed and worked with all their hearts.

On the appointed day, they both appeared before the pope. "You may begin, Brother Thomas," said Urban IV.

Thomas read out all the hymns, prayers, and texts he had composed. They were so magnificent that Bonaventure and the pope were overwhelmed. There was a moment of silence before Urban at last said, "Your turn now, Brother Bonaventure!"

At that, the saintly monk threw himself at the pope's feet, crying out, "Holy Father, as I listened to Brother Thomas, I felt as though I was hearing the Holy Spirit himself! He alone could have inspired such beautiful words. Here, look at what remains of my feeble efforts."

And, opening the folds of his habit, he let fall a shower of confetti—his own writings that he'd ripped to shreds as he listened to his friend speak.

It is said that the pope praised Bonaventure's humility as much as Thomas' genius. Many years later both Thomas and Bonaventure were declared saints.

On June 19, 1264, the pope led a solemn procession of the Blessed Sacrament. And, for the first time, the magnificent hymns composed by Saint Thomas Aquinas rose up to heaven, just as they still do today at the ceremonies and the processions in honor of the Eucharist.

# Fire! Fire!

On the Monday after Pentecost in 1608, the abbey bells in Faverney, France, were chiming three o'clock in the morning. The monks awoke and headed to the church for Matins, the prayers said in the earliest hours of the day.

As usual, the sacristan took the big church key out of his pocket. As he opened the door, thick smoke stung his eyes and filled his lungs.

"Fire! Fire!" he cried out in horror.

Flames crackled around the altar where the Blessed Sacrament was exposed in a beautiful silver monstrance. The monks came running, as well as some villagers roused from their sleep by the cries.

"Quick, quick, bring buckets of water! Hurry!"

They formed a chain to pass the buckets. By the first rays of dawn, the fire had been put out. But the church had suffered much damage.

The marble altar was in ruins, and the brass candlesticks had melted. Nothing was left of the sumptuous fabrics that had hung in the sanctuary.

"But where's the monstrance with the consecrated host?" the father prior gravely asked. Everyone searched through the rubble where the altar had been. Suddenly, Antoine Hudelot, a young novice only thirteen years old, pointed his finger in the air. "There it is, look!"

Indeed, the monstrance, with the host clearly visible, was there above them, at the same height where they had placed it the night before. Though everything beneath it had been destroyed, it was hovering in midair all on its own! The sacristan was about to grab it, but a monk held him back: "Don't you see, it's a miracle!"

They all gathered around to gaze in amazement at the monstrance defying the law of gravity!

News of the miracle spread like wildfire through the town. The people of Faverney came to help clean up the church, but, above all, to see this extraordinary wonder with their own eyes. There were soon so many people, they were jostling each other.

Workmen carried in a long plank of wood to hold back the crowd. But as they did so, they accidentally bumped it into the choir gate right near the monstrance.

"Watch out!" someone yelled. "You're going to knock it down!"

The gate rattled and swung shut with a loud bang, but the monstrance didn't budge an inch!

Soon groups of people were arriving from the neighboring villages. The miracle continued as, with awe and admiration, the visitors contemplated the monstrance suspended in midair.

Some Capuchin monks nearby, renowned for their scholarship and holiness, were informed of the miracle, and they came to examine the extraordinary phenomenon. One of them had a stick, then a cloth passed all around the monstrance. But no, there was nothing attached to it, nothing holding it in place. There was no other explanation for the midair monstrance than the hand of God!

During that whole day of Pentecost Monday, right into the night, a steady stream of the faithful came to pray with all their heart before the hovering monstrance. The news also drew the simply curious, like one man who recounted, "I couldn't believe my eyes—I went in and out of the church more than thirty times to look at it, trying, if it were possible, to understand such a miracle. In the end, I prayed to God to enlighten me, and I understood that a monstrance couldn't remain hanging in the air like that without some supernatural power."

"When and how will this end?" everyone was wondering.

The next day, around ten o'clock in the morning, the curate of a neighboring village, who had come with his parishioners to see the miracle, was celebrating Mass in the church. At the very moment he pronounced the words of consecration, the monstrance very gently descended on its own to the temporary altar that had been set up below it!

And so the miracle ended, after about thirty-three hours, and after thousands of people had witnessed it.

The archbishop of Besançon, France, ordered a very thorough investigation. It concluded that this was an authentic miracle, which Pope Pius IX later confirmed. In 1908, splendid celebrations were held for the third centenary of the miracle in the church of Faverney, which had since become a basilica.

This miracle made such an impression on people that, soon thereafter, a drawing of the monstrance could be found engraved on walls or furniture in almost every home in the region.

# Saint Margaret Mary Alacoque

"**O**h, that Sister Margaret Mary has always got her head in the clouds," said several annoyed sisters at the Convent of the Visitation in Paray-le-Monial, France, where the young nun had just made her perpetual vows.

"She's kind to everyone and always ready to be of help, but she often seems off in a world of her own!" remarked Sister Jeanne de Chantal to the superior. "For example, Mother Superior, today she was asked to tend two donkeys in the meadow while we were gardening. And later we found her on her knees praying in the middle of the field! With no one to watch them, the two little donkeys got into the vegetable patch. It's a miracle they didn't eat anything!"

"No doubt the prayers of Sister Margaret Mary stopped them!" replied Mother Superior, who knew the young nun to be a model of humility and obedience.

It's true that Sister Margaret Mary never stopped praying, but she also made an effort to work hard. She agreed with a smile to do the sweeping or the laundry whenever she was asked, and she did it well.

December 27, 1673, was the feast day of Saint John the Evangelist. The Blessed Sacrament was exposed on the main altar of the convent chapel, in a lovely golden monstrance. Sister Margaret Mary was there, unmoving and peaceful, in adoration before the host. It was then she had her first great vision of Jesus.

"He held me to his holy breast a long time as he revealed to me the wonders of his love and the inexplicable secrets of his Sacred Heart," she wrote a little later.

"My Sacred Heart so burns with love for mankind, it cannot contain all its ardent flames," Jesus told her. "Someone must help spread those flames of charity."

Jesus chose Sister Margaret Mary as his instrument to remind all people just how much he loves them.

A little later, Jesus appeared to her again. This time he asked her to pray with him for an hour during the night of Thursday to Friday, in memory of his agony in the garden of Gethsemane.

But the next day, when Sister Margaret Mary told Mother Superior of this request, she said, "What stories have you dreamed up this time? I forbid it!"

She and the other nuns did not believe Sister Margaret Mary, and some of the nuns began teasing her.

Fortunately, with the arrival of the convent's new chaplain, Father Claude La Colombière, Sister Margaret Mary found support. This priest understood that Jesus had truly entrusted her with a mission.

On June 13, 1675, the feast of Corpus Christi, the young nun was again praying before the Eucharist. Jesus appeared to her, standing and pointing to his heart, which was as though encircled by the flames of his love and crowned with thorns.

He said to her, "Behold this Heart, which has so loved men that it spared nothing, even going so far as to give itself completely to prove to them its love. And in return I receive from most people nothing but ingratitude, contempt, and irreverence, especially in the way they treat me in this Sacrament of Love."

Poor Jesus! He went on, "I so thirst to be honored and loved in the Blessed Sacrament, but I find hardly anyone willing to slake that thirst."

Jesus also asked for a special feast day in honor of his Sacred Heart, and he made wonderful promises of graces and blessings for all those who would receive Communion on the first Friday of each month for nine months.

Thanks to Father La Colombière, little by little, Saint Margaret Mary's message was taken seriously, and the insistent request of Jesus was finally fulfilled.

The feast of the Sacred Heart is now celebrated the world over on the third Friday after Pentecost. More and more of the faithful come to adore Jesus present in the Eucharist, to respond to his love with trust and simplicity of heart.

# Secret Mass in a French Forest

"Hey, is everything okay up there?" Victor shouted. "Is everything quiet?"

"Yes, yes, shush! Everything's fine," replied Mathurin.

Right at the top of an oak tree, this strapping young fellow was on the lookout. Through the branches, he could make out in the distance the arms of the windmill in the shape of an X. That was the all-clear signal, no sign of government soldiers. For the moment, they were safe. But they still had to be on their guard.

It was the time of the French Revolution. After the first celebrations of freedom, what became known as the Reign of Terror had set in. Churches were closed and public worship forbidden. Priests, and many of their parishioners, were hunted down. Even nuns were killed. But in a small pocket in the west of France, the Vendée, the faithful resisted the anti-Catholic government and went into hiding.

That day, everyone was busy in the forest getting ready for the Easter Mass that would soon take place. How they longed to receive the Risen Lord in the Eucharist!

"Oh, what a beautiful ray of sunshine!" cried Madame Louise. "I hope it's a good sign of peace to come."

What ordeals these poor people had suffered. They had fled in haste from many of the surrounding villages, all destroyed by fire as their neighbors were brutally massacred by French soldiers. The winter of 1793–1794 had been very tough in the forest, with the snow, the endless rain, and the prowling wolves.

Celeste, who three months· ago had seen her two little children killed before her eyes, came out of her hut built of branches. She was carrying a large white linen sheet.

"Here you are, for the altar."

She walked over to the big plank set on logs, which would be used for Mass, and spread the sheet carefully on top. Bits of candle were placed on top, ready to be lit before Mass began.

The makeshift altar was set up in an outdoor chapel made of woven branches. The ground around it was carpeted with braided heather.

Marie and Victorine, two eight-year-olds, arrived with a pretty bunch of flowers they'd picked in the forest and placed garlands of ferns all around the altar.

"How beautiful!" exclaimed Jeannette, who not so long ago had been smuggling secret messages in her lace bonnet for the soldiers of the resistance.

Etienne the blacksmith shouted in a loud voice, "Jacques, you stand guard there, where the path starts, with your sickle. And you, Pierre and Henri, you be on the lookout near the well. You know the signal if there's any danger."

All was ready; the people had only to await the brave priest who had gone into hiding on the farms and in the woods, bringing solace and sacraments to the faithful. At last he came out of the little hut where he had been hearing confessions for most of the night.

"Wait a moment longer, my dear children," he said. "Before beginning Mass, I must go see that poor soldier who arrived last night. Say a prayer for him, for he is surely soon to join our dear Lord in heaven!"

The priest quickly set out for the hut that served as their field hospital. There he found Marie Maindron nursing the wounded man. A courageous resistance fighter, he had been stabbed twice in the chest with a bayonet, just above the image of the Sacred Heart that was sown onto his jacket. He was very pale, and his breathing was very shallow.

"The surgeon visited during the night," Marie whispered.

The priest administered last rites to the wounded man and held his hand as he prayed over him for a few moments.

Then he went out and celebrated Easter Mass. There were no bells to proclaim the Resurrection of Jesus, unless you count the bell on their one remaining cow, but those gathered sang out with all their hearts and were very fervent indeed.

Father could always find the words to comfort and console all these sorely tested peasants. To put the joy of Easter into their hearts, he said, "My very dear friends, stay brave. Jesus triumphed over death; he rose again. He has taken to his Heart all the martyrs in our families, and he is very close to each one of you!"

The congregation advanced to the altar to receive Communion. How lovely it was to see all these faces, young and old, who had survived so many trials, looking up with tears in their eyes, their hearts burning with love for Jesus in the Blessed Sacrament!

Sunlight flooded the forest. Comforted by the Bread of heaven, all together the people concluded the Mass in song: "We know Christ is truly risen from the dead! To us, victorious King, have mercy! Alleluia, alleluia!"

The hymn mingled with the sudden cries of a newborn, brought in the arms of his godmother to be baptized. The baby's name was Louis. The son of the coachman, he had been born a few days earlier in the forest that hid so many mysteries and secrets.

On this Easter morning, in the heart of the tortured French Vendée, the new life offered by Jesus Christ shone brightly!

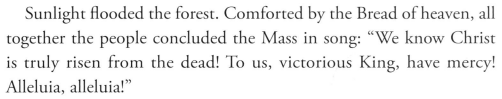

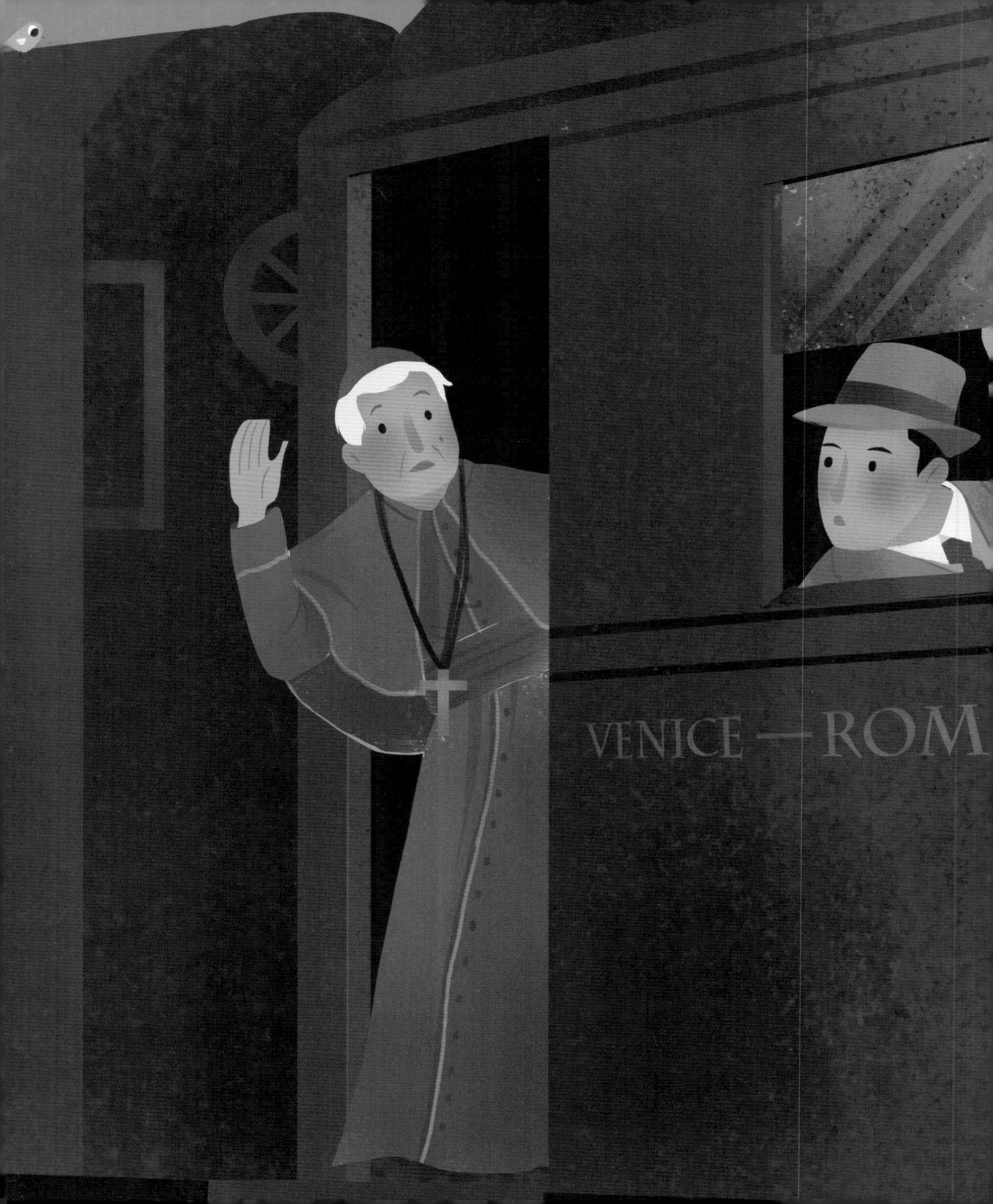
VENICE — ROM

# Saint Pius X, the Pope of the Blessed Sacrament

The sisters of Cardinal Sarto, archbishop of Venice, were busy carefully packing his suitcase, making sure he hadn't forgotten anything.

"I don't need that many things for a trip to Rome; it's not like I'm going on a world tour!" he jokingly teased them.

Once at the train station, Cardinal Sarto went to the ticket counter: "I would like a round-trip ticket to Rome, please."

Cardinal Sarto was going to take part in the election of a new pope to succeed Leo XIII, who had just died. Little did he know he would never use the return part of that ticket, for it was he who would be elected pope on August 4, 1903!

Shortly after his election, as Pope Pius X, he surprised the world by his simplicity and his sense of humor. One day, he slipped into the Vatican gardens to take a walk on his own, without an escort. He watched as the mounted guards, concerned by his disappearance, set off on their horses at high speed in search of him. He later recounted with a laugh, "They chased me down like a prime suspect in a manhunt!"

This free-spirited new pope introduced many reforms and novelties into the Church in order to "restore all things in Christ"—for that, indeed, was his motto.

He wished seminaries to become schools of knowledge and virtue to train truly saintly priests; he wished for a beautiful liturgy with hymns that would move hearts and would be easy to learn and understand.

And, he, who so loved Jesus present in the Blessed Sacrament, told all Christians, "Receive Communion frequently, even daily if possible."

Pope Pius X recalled the words of Jesus, who compared the Bread of heaven, the Eucharist, to the manna that had rained down each day to feed the Hebrews in the desert.

The pope never forgot how he had suffered as a child, having to wait until he was eleven to make his First Communion, as was the custom at the time. He turned old habits on their head by deciding that, from then on, children could receive Communion as soon as they were able to understand the difference between a consecrated host and ordinary bread.

"Let the little children come," he said, "and do not hinder them from being seated at the table of the Lord!"

That was almost a revolution, but above all it was a source of great joy throughout the Church!

And thus it was that, in April 1912, an unusual pilgrimage took place in Rome.

Four hundred French youngsters traveled from France. The seven- and eight-year-olds had recently made their First Communion and wanted to thank the pope for being allowed to receive Jesus at their age.

Along with their parents and schoolteachers, they met with the Holy Father at the Vatican. Then the priest who had organized the pilgrimage said a few words: "Holy Father, over the course of history, emperors and kings have come to Rome to kneel at the feet of Saint Peter's successor. Knights and crusaders have asked him to bless their weapons, but this is the first time that a crusade of First Communicants has come to thank the sovereign pontiff in his palace in Rome."

The young pilgrims were invited to attend the pope's Mass. What joy for them to receive Communion from the pope's own hands and then to speak with him very simply, as kids talk to their dads! Pius X gave a short speech in French. "Through Communion," he said, "become, each one of you, a real little apostle of Jesus! Have you understood my French all right?"

"Oh, yes, Holy Father!" cried all the children—all except one little girl, who was so moved by the simplicity and kindness of the pope that she blurted out, "Oh, yes, Jesus!"

Soon afterward, a young mother presented her little son to Pius X to receive his blessing. When the little boy went up to him, the pope asked him, "How old are you?"

"He's four," replied his mom. "I hope he will make his First Communion in two years."

Pius looked into the child's bright eyes for a long moment. Then he asked him, "What does one receive in Holy Communion?"

"Jesus, of course!" replied the little boy without hesitation.

"And who is Jesus?" asked the pope.

"He's the good Lord."

"Bring him to me tomorrow morning," said the Holy Father with a gentle smile. "I will give him his First Communion myself!"

At his canonization Mass, Pope Pius XII proclaimed Saint Pius X "the pope of the Blessed Sacrament," and he is still known by this lovely title to this day. Thanks to him, children the world over can receive the Body of Christ.

# The Secret Ordination at Dachau

It was the middle of World War II in Germany, and, just like every other week, Mädi flew along for more than six miles on her bike, her lovely blonde braids dancing joyfully on the breeze. In secret, and at great risk, this fearless little girl was carrying a little food and comfort to the prisoners of the Dachau concentration camp. From time to time, through the thick barbed wire, she could see some of the inmates, dressed in a kind of striped pajamas, their heads shaved, and looking pale, worn out, and haggard. She could spot them working in a big greenhouse, where they grew vegetables and flowers. A little hut served as a sales desk.

One day, while the sentry wasn't looking, Mädi was able to gain the trust of one prisoner, Stanislaw, a young Polish priest who served at the counter. From then on Mädi would buy a bunch of flowers and then secretly pass him some bread and ham—and sometimes letters.

Father Stanislaw was always so full of thanks: "Oh, thank you, Mädi!"

Then, one day, he added in a whisper, "Could you bring us some hosts, so the priests can celebrate Mass? We do it in secret, while the men are working in the greenhouse."

"Yes, of course!" At the risk of her own life, Mädi would do anything she could to make the Eucharistic Jesus present for these believers detained in such inhuman conditions.

Among the prisoners was Karl Leisner, a young German deacon. Already ill when he arrived at Dachau, he was lying between life and death in the camp infirmary. He had so dreamed of his ordination, which would make him a priest for all eternity! How he longed to give the Body and the Blood of the Lord to his faithful who were suffering so greatly during this time of war.  But, alas, he was surely soon to die.

When a new convoy of prisoners arrived, among them was Bishop Gabriel Piguet from France. "Perhaps he could ordain you, Karl!" suggested one of the prisoners working in the infirmary.

"Ordained in Dachau?" Karl cried. "That's unthinkable!"

And yet, the idea grew and grew on Karl, who was now at the end of his strength.  One day, he finally wrote to his bishop to ask permission to be ordained at Dachau.

So it was that one winter's day, on arriving at the prison greenhouse, Mädi learned that a very important mission awaited her: to deliver Karl's letter to Bishop Clemens von Galen.

But how to organize an ordination Mass, a solemn celebration of the Blessed Sacrament, in a concentration camp under such tight surveillance?

Karl's bishop responded immediately: "I authorize the requested ordination on condition that it be properly carried out and attested in writing."

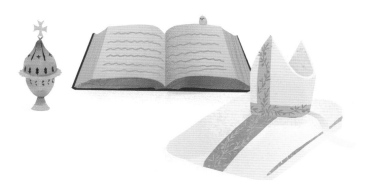

A few days later Bishop von Galen was instructing Mädi, "Here is the holy oil for the anointing, the text for the rite of ordination, and a stole."

You can just imagine how eagerly Mädi was awaited at the camp! When she arrived with her precious and carefully hidden cargo, she learned with joy that the ordination was to take place the following Sunday, December 17, 1944.

As the clandestine ordination was prepared, all of the prisoners, whatever their religion, wholeheartedly took part! In the mechanics' workshop, a Russian Orthodox man made an episcopal ring out of brass for Bishop Piguet. On the ring he engraved the words "Our Lady of Dachau." A German Trappist monk secretly carved a beautiful oak cross. Some Protestant inmates made a superb miter of silk embroidered with pearls, which they managed to stitch at night without any guards noticing.

By December 17, everything was ready. Outside, despite the cold, an old Jewish prisoner played the violin to distract the guards' attention.

Karl was burning with fever and seated on a stool, for he had no more strength left. But his face was beaming with joy! In a moving ceremony, Bishop Piguet pronounced the ritual words, and Karl became a priest of Jesus Christ. Around them, in their tattered rags, a group of priests and seminarians softly chanted beautiful hymns before laying their hands on the newly ordained priest. Heaven had truly descended on the wretched camp!

Printed in September 2020, in Malaysia.
Job number MGN 20035-02
Printed in compliance with
the Consumer Protection Safety Act, 2008